T0011800

What's Your Money Personality?

VISTA®
HIGHER LEARNING

Boston, Massachusetts

SOCIAL STUDIES

pay for food

activity

money

Everyone needs money. It's very important. In fact, it would be very difficult to live without money. We need it for lots of different things. Of course, we need it to pay for the food we eat. We also need it to pay for our activities and other things. We simply need it to live. It's the same for everyone. However, we don't all use money the same way. People have very different ideas about money!

What do people do with their money? This answer varies a great deal from person to person. We all use the money we have differently. We all have different **money personalities**.

A money personality is a way of thinking. It shows how a person feels about money. It explains what each person does with his or her money. Your money personality can tell you a lot about you *and* your spending!

It's a fact of life that everyone spends money. We spend money on many different things. We spend it on clothes. We spend it on fun activities. We spend it on all the things we need. But how much do you spend? And what do you buy? That's where your money personality comes in!

Big Spender

expensive

$$$

Take a look at this guy for example. He likes to buy **expensive** things. It's always the newest and the best for him! He has a big expensive car. He always has the **latest** cell phone and he buys a new computer every year. He wants people to see that he always has the best things. He's a "**big spender**!"

People who are big spenders just love buying very nice things. They choose the newest and most expensive clothes. They choose to eat the most expensive foods. They always want the best **goods and services**—even if they aren't **worth** it. Why? Having expensive things makes these people feel important. Big spenders want to enjoy their money today. They don't always think about tomorrow. Do you know any big spenders?

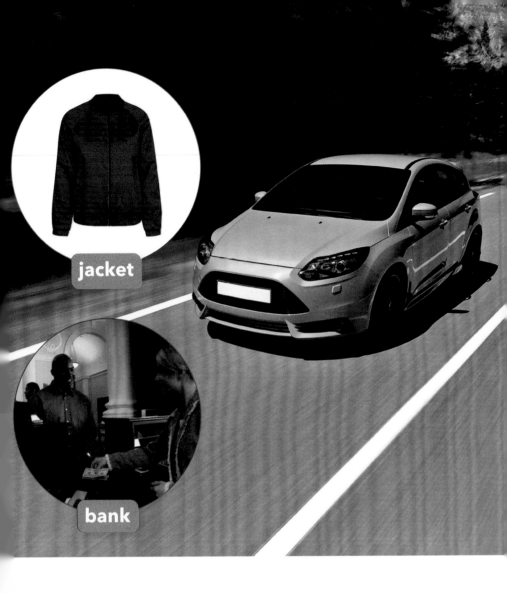

jacket

bank

There are also people who think it's important to save money for the future. These people are "**savers**." There are many different reasons a saver may put money away. For example, the person may want to save money to buy a car. Perhaps he or she wants to save money to buy a cool new jacket. Some savers just like to have money in the bank. You never know what might happen. Savers think it's always good to **be prepared**!

Saver

Take this person, for example. Her money personality is very different from a big spender. In fact, she's the complete opposite! She's a saver, but that doesn't mean that she never spends money. The important thing for her is that she spends less than she **earns**. She's happy to use an old phone. She has great clothes, but they're not new. She's completely OK with that!

2030 Calendar

future

$18

price

Savers are very careful with money. They're the kind of people who make **budgets**. They generally only go shopping when they need something. When they're shopping, they check the prices of things to be sure they get a **good deal**. They also often look for free or **cheap** activities to do.

Savers have money, but it's usually in the bank. They don't enjoy spending. They enjoy having money for the future.

Now let's look at another example of a money personality. The person you see here is a "**shopper**." Can you guess what shoppers like to do? They like to shop, of course!

Shoppers are people who like going to stores. They like looking for new things to buy, even if they don't really need them. They just like buying a lot of stuff!

Shopper

store

Shoppers feel good when they're looking for things to buy. They like the feeling of finding and buying something new. The problem is, there is always something new to buy! What a shopper buys today may not make him or her happy tomorrow!

Shoppers don't always buy expensive things. In fact, they often look for great deals. They just love shopping so much that they often buy *a lot*. Sometimes they even buy things they don't need!

Avoider

He avoids thinking about money. He tries not to do it.

Now let's learn about a very different money personality: the "**avoider**." Avoiders may have money, or they may not. Sometimes they don't even know how much money they have! Why? Avoiders don't like to think about money at all. It makes them uncomfortable, so they avoid thinking about it.

For avoiders, money is something they don't really understand. It just makes them worried, and they find it a real bother. As a result, they avoid dealing with it completely.

bill

This person is an example of an avoider. She has some money in the bank, but how much? She has no idea! She isn't planning to do anything with it. She doesn't **keep track of** how much money she uses either. When she gets a **bill**, instead of checking it and paying it, she puts it away and tries to forget about it. Does she plan for the future? No way! It's too much work for her!

Which money personality are you?

Take our test to find out.

1. You feel bored. What do you do?

A go shopping

B do an activity that is free

C look at magazines for new things to buy

D go out or stay home, whichever I want

2. You're hungry. There's no food at home. What do you do?

A go shopping at the mall and get food there

B go to the supermarket and cook something at home

C find a new cool restaurant to try

D get food at the nearest place no matter what it costs

3. What's a good present to give?

A any cool thing I see in stores

B a present I made at home

C something new and expensive

D whatever the person wants

4. What do you usually do when shopping?

A look for new things to buy

B make a list first and only buy things on it

C buy the best and the newest things I see

D buy what I want and don't look at prices

5. You have some extra money. What will you do with it?

A go shopping

B put it in the bank

C buy the newest video game system because yours is a year old

D leave it where it is

What's your spending personality?

Your answers are . . .

mostly A: You usually aren't very careful with money.
You're a shopper.

mostly B: You usually are careful with money.
You're a saver.

mostly C: You like mostly nice and expensive things.
You're a big spender.

mostly D: You don't like thinking about money.
You're an avoider.

money personality the way a person thinks about and uses money

expensive costing a lot of money

latest the newest or most recent; e.g., *He has the latest cell phone. It just came out last week.*

big spender an expression for someone who buys costly things or does costly activities, often to seem important

goods and services goods are things you can buy; services are systems that provide useful help like delivery services or offering meals in a restaurant

worth having a value in money; e.g., *The coat is worth $135.*

saver an expression for someone who likes to put money in a bank account or keep it for a later time

be prepared to be ready for something

earn to get money for working

budget to make plans for how to spend money

good deal having good value for the money needed to buy something

cheap costing very little

shopper an expression for someone who buys things just because he or she likes the feeling spending money gives

avoider an expression for someone who tries to stay away from money because he or she finds it a bother

keep track of to watch for regular information about something

bill a piece of paper that shows how much to pay